LEGENDS

OF

STOCKPORT
COUNTY FC

Written and compiled by Guy M

CW00551436

at heart publications

Manchester
EveningNews

Stockport
Express

First published in 2008 by
At Heart Ltd
32 Stamford Street
Altrincham
Cheshire
WA14 1EY

in conjunction with
Manchester Evening News
1 Scott Place
Hardman Street
Manchester
M3 3RN

All images kindly supplied by Manchester Evening News, Stockport Express and Stockport County FC.

© 2008 Manchester Evening News

All rights reserved. No part of this book may be reproduced in any form or by any means, including information storage and retrieval systems without permission in writing from the publisher, except by a reviewer who may quote passages in a review.

ISBN: 978-1-84547-195-8

Printed and bound by Ashford Colour Press, Gosport.

CONTENTS

The achievements of Dave Jones's promotion-winning side in 1996/97 drew thousands of fans on to the streets of Stockport to acknowledge their heroes' success.

INTRODUCTION

Stockport County began celebrating their 125th anniversary as a football club at the start of 2008.

Inevitably, that means many fans have been looking back down the years, focusing on the championships, promotions and Cup runs that the team has enjoyed. The individuals who played in those successful teams certainly deserve to be remembered, but even in the dark days of applying for re-election, players have emerged worthy of adulation.

The idea of County having legends to call their own might strike a non-supporter as a little far-fetched. After all, this is a club that has all too often found itself stranded at the wrong end of the Football League. But the truth is there are many names that have resounded down the years – Alf Lythgoe, Jack Connor and Bill

Bocking are all known to County fans even though most are too young to have seen them play.

In fact, the problem in compiling this list has been who to leave out rather than scratching around for names worthy of the title 'legend'. The club launched its own Hall of Fame in 2002, providing the basis for this list of players, who received their share of adulation down the years.

Legends of Stockport County FC is a fascinating collection of photographs of County's greatest players. It's your chance to discover the fans' favourites from more than a century of football in Stockport.

Guy Nelson
Manchester Evening News

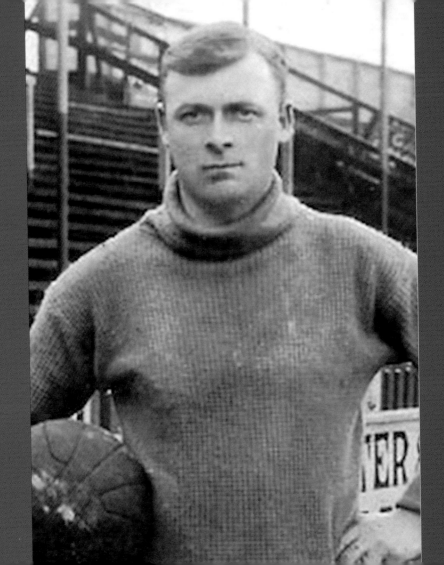

Joe BUTLER

This former miner took over in goal in County's first season in the Football League in 1900.

Butler quickly became a fans' favourite for his bravery and skill, keeping County in with a chance in their difficult first few years in the League. In one famous game on 19 April 1902, when only seven players started against Chesterfield, four having missed the train, it was only Butler's heroics that kept the score down to 8-1!

After three seasons of re-election, County lost their place in the League at the end of the 1904 season, but Butler stayed loyal and helped them to first place in the Lancashire Combination in the following campaign.

After a brief spell with Clapton Orient, Butler returned to Edgeley Park for two seasons before switching to Glossop. He then moved to Sunderland with whom he won a First Division championship medal and also an FA Cup runners-up medal.

He returned to County in 1916 for a third spell to play three seasons in the wartime league.

1900 - 1905, 1906 - 1908

Arther WHARTON

The first black footballer in the world to turn professional ended his career at Stockport County. Wharton was born in the Gold Coast (now Ghana), and at the age of 20 had set a world record of 10 seconds for a 100-yard sprint.

As a goalkeeper, he played for Darlington, Preston North End, Rotherham Town, Sheffield United, Stalybridge Rovers, Ashton North End and Stalybridge again before joining County at the start of the 1901 season.

He played only six times in Division Two, conceding 16 goals. He worked in a Yorkshire colliery for the final 15 years of his life, dying in 1930.

1901 - 1902

Harry HARDY

Harry Hardy remains the only player to win a full England cap while with County. The hometown goalkeeper kept a clean sheet against Belgium at the Hawthorns on 8 December 1924.

He also represented the Football League against the Irish League that same year, and played in five Tests in a Football League representative side that toured Australia in March 1925. In the 1921/22 Division Three (North) championship season, he kept a remarkable 23 clean sheets with County.

Everton took him to Goodison Park for £2,350 in October 1925 and Hardy played six times when they won the First Division title in 1928. He ended his career with Bury.

1919 - 1925

Ted CRITCHLEY

County would never have been forgiven if they'd missed out on the talent of outside-right Ted Critchley. After all, he was right under their noses.

Spotted playing for Cheadle Lads in a game on St Lesmo Road, just around the corner from Edgeley Park, he was quickly snapped up. The skillful winger came into his own in Division Two, but after County were relegated in 1926 he was transferred to Everton for £3,000.

In his first full season at Goodison Park, Critchley was part of the Everton side that won the First Division Championship in 1928, providing many of the crosses that Dixie Dean headed home in his record 60 goals.

After bouncing back from relegation Critchley and Everton won another First Division championship in 1932. He moved on to Preston North End and Port Vale before returning to his home town at the end of his career.

Bill BOCKING

Local lad Bocking was hugely respected in the game for the skill and strength he brought to his role as right-back and County captain in the 1920s and '30s.

He made 276 appearances for the club he joined from Hyde United in 1923 before moving on to Everton in 1931 for a four-figure sum. However, he failed to carve out a regular spot for the Toffees and returned to County in 1934.

In his penultimate season as a player, Bocking was part of the side that secured County the Division Three (North) title in 1937, but missed the final victory against Lincoln City in front of 27,000 fans at Edgeley Park through injury.

Unfortunately, Bocking's name is also forever linked with a fifth-round FA Cup defeat by West Bromwich Albion on 16 February 1935. As skipper, and having won the toss, Bocking elected to play into a gale-force wind and by half-time County were 5-0 down, which turned out to be the final score.

1923 - 1931, 1934 - 1938

Harry BURGESS

Another example of County's ability to foster goal-scoring talent in the 1920s, Alderley Edge-born Burgess arrived at Edgeley Park as an amateur from Nantwich Ramblers.

Burgess scored 72 goals in 121 appearances for the Hatters, convincing Sheffield Wednesday to pay £3,000 for him in June 1929 – a record for County at the time. The powerful inside-forward went on to win a championship with Wednesday and earn four England caps before moving on to Chelsea.

Burgess returned to play seven times more for County as a guest during the war.

1925 - 1929

Billy NEWTON

During Billy Newton's four seasons as a wing-half for the Hatters, he provided the service for the club's prolific scorers Joe Smith, Harry Burgess and Frank Newton.

Newton had begun his playing career with Blyth Spartans after working in the town's shipyards. Spells at Newcastle United and Cardiff City provided him with little chance of first-team football before he switched to Leicester City, Grimsby Town and then Stockport County.

After his 160 League and Cup appearances for County he moved on to Hull City, but returned to Edgeley Park in 1932 to take on roles as player-coach with the third team and then reserve team manager. Fred Westgarth made him senior trainer in 1934, a position he held for 30 years.

Billy Newton and Jimmy Stevenson received a joint testimonial in 1969.

1927 - 1931

Frank NEWTON

The big centre-forward, who was born in Romiley in 1902, made certain County would not forget him when he watched them training while still an Ashton United player at the start of 1928. Every time the ball came his way he returned it with such power that manager Lincoln Hyde signed him up.

In the 1929/30 season Newton scored 38 goals in 38 games, including five in one game and three hat-tricks. He followed that remarkable record up with another 37 goals in 41 appearances the following season.

Such goal-scoring heroics brought him to the attention of Fulham, who took him to Craven Cottage for £575 where he continued his remarkable record of almost a goal per game.

Newton moved to Reading and back to Fulham before a broken leg called a halt to his playing career. Newton finished his League career, which lasted just seven years, with the figures of 192 goals in 209 games.

1928 - 1931

Jimmy STEVENSON

The Scottish inside-forward played his part when County created a Football League record that still stands to this day. On 6 January 1934, County put 13 goals past Halifax Town at Edgeley Park without reply, and Stevenson scored two of these.

Stevenson had arrived from non-League Aldershot following spells with Third Lanark, South Shields and Bradford City. At County, he became part of a formidable attacking side that included Alf Lythgoe, Percy Downes, Jabez Foulkes and later Joe Hill.

After a ligament problem ended his playing career he managed Macclesfield Town before returning to Edgeley Park as reserve team trainer. He spent another 35 years at County in various capacities and in 2002 was enrolled into the club's Hall of Fame.

1932 - 1935

Alf LYTHGOE

The idea of a modern-day striker scoring 80 goals from 69 League starts beggars belief. But that's exactly what Alf Lythgoe did in his first spell with County in the 1930s.

Standing just 5ft 7ins tall, Lythgoe had been released by Crewe Alexandra before drifting into non-League football in his native Cheshire. County took him from Ashton National in June 1932 and, after a slow start, Lythgoe repaid their faith.

He scored 46 League goals in 39 appearances – plus six more in Cup competitions – in the 1933/34 season, including five hat-tricks and two in the record 13-0 victory over Halifax Town. He hit five in the 6-1 victory over Southport on the opening day of the following season and was bought by Huddersfield in the October for £3,500.

A successful spell at Leeds Road ended in March 1938 when he was transferred back to County, but couldn't help prevent his old side being relegated to the Third Division (North). Despite scoring another 20 goals he was released in the summer of 1939, but not before he had confirmed his legendary status.

1932 - 1934, 1938 - 1939

Pre-1950s

Duggie REID

Gentle giant Duggie Reid joined County from amateur side Heaton Chapel FC in 1934. He had left his native Ayrshire after taking a job as an apprentice plumber in Manchester when he was just 15 years old.

Reid was part of the County side that took the Third Division (North) title in 1937, but as a second-choice centre-forward he missed the championship decider against Lincoln City.

Switching to wing-half the following season, Reid began to attract attention for his dynamic runs and his devastating free kicks, the power of which had not been seen before at Edgeley Park. Reid also made sporadic wartime appearances for the club, when he wasn't away serving with the army.

In 1946 County received a record £7,000 fee for 28-year-old Reid from Portsmouth, where he became a folk hero as Pompey brought consecutive First Division championships in 1948/49 and 1949/50 to Fratton Park.

 1954 - 1964

1950s

Jack CONNOR

Legendary goal-scorer Jack Connor was pushing 30 by the time he arrived at Edgeley Park, and anxious to make up for lost time. Having endured unmemorable stints with Ipswich Town and Carlisle United, he started rattling in the goals for Rochdale at the rate of one every two games.

Connor signed for County from Bradford City in October 1951 for £2,500, after manager Andy Beattie, determined to get his man, tracked him to a Bradford cinema to make sure he put pen to paper. Connor, with a rare ability to shoot with either foot, scored more than 30 goals in each of the four full seasons he spent at the club.

With 17 hat-tricks in the 140 goals he scored for County, it was no surprise that in a special poll by County's Ex-Players' Association in 2000 to find out the Hatters' Player of the Century, Connor came way out on top.

1951 - 1956

1950s

Bryan 'Boy' BRENNAN

County's greatest-ever schoolboy footballer was given a rapturous reception when he and his remaining Stockport Boys teammates paraded their 1948 English Schools Trophy around Edgeley Park 60 years later in April 2008.

Brennan's name has passed into the folklore of the club despite the fact he only ever played four full League games for County. An orphan from Stockport's Barnes Industrial School, his excellent scoring record brought him six England Schoolboys caps. He made his name in 1947/48 when the Stockport Boys side beat all-comers until two draws with Liverpool Boys (the first leg in front of 25,000 fans at Edgeley Park) made Brennan's side joint-holders of the English Schoolboys Trophy.

Brennan's profile at the time was such that he was pictured on the cover of the Hotspur Book of Football Stars for 1948/49 alongside Stan Mortensen. But despite signing for County he was only given the briefest of runs in the first team at the end of the 1950/51 season due, in the main, to two years' National Service.

1951

1950s

Bobby MURRAY

The Scottish half-back played 465 League appearances for County – a record that would only be surpassed by Andy Thorpe in 1991.

Murray, who gave up a career on the railways north of the border to try his luck with County, was a smart player in a side that never really attained glory before slipping down into the Fourth Division in 1959.

He was capable of playing in a variety of positions, as he did in a memorable run of 226 consecutive League and Cup games between August 1954 and February 1959. In all, he scored 32 goals in 495 League and Cup games for County.

1952 - 1963

1950s

Ray DRAKE

Local boy Drake secured his place in the record books with County's fastest-ever goal. It took him just seven seconds to net against Accrington Stanley on Christmas Day 1956!

Drake had suffered meningitis as a child, which left him completely deaf in one ear with restricted hearing in the other. But his determination to succeed, and the benefits of having a County-supporting boss at the Co-op, led to a trial at Edgeley Park while playing for Bramhall.

He spent three years in the reserves before being called up by the first team, for which he scored 19 goals in 22 games, including four against Wrexham on 23 February 1957. Suggestions of a possible swap deal with Bolton for Nat Lofthouse showed how far Drake's star had risen, but that never materialised, and a disagreement with boss Willie Moir led to Drake leaving the club.

He opted to remain living in Stockport, so chose a move to Altrincham rather than signing for a League club further afield. His final total of 234 goals for County in 201 games at all levels remains a fantastic achievement.

Pictured left: Ray Drake scores for County on his debut in the 3-0 victory over Derby County on 1 December 1956.

1956 - 1957

County boss Trevor Porteous was all smiles at the prospect of a big pay-day for the club after 18,000 tickets were sold in just four hours for the FA Cup replay with Liverpool in February 1965.

A man for all seasons, Trevor Porteous arrived as a promising defender from Hull City in 1956 and enjoyed a 41-year association with County until his death in 1997.

Porteous made 364 appearances for County, but he is equally remembered for his spell as player-manager from September 1963 to May 1965. County finished bottom of the Fourth Division in 1964/65 and were forced to apply for re-election for the first time in more than 50 years. But the same season also saw one of County's most famous Cup exploits, drawing 1-1 at Liverpool in the fourth round of the FA Cup before losing the replay 2-0 at Edgeley Park.

Porteous was sacked two months into the following season, but later returned as assistant manager to Jimmy Meadows, seeing County promoted from the Fourth Division as champions in 1967. He spent seven years as club physio and also served as groundsman, scout and youth team manager for the club he loved.

1956 - 1965

1960s

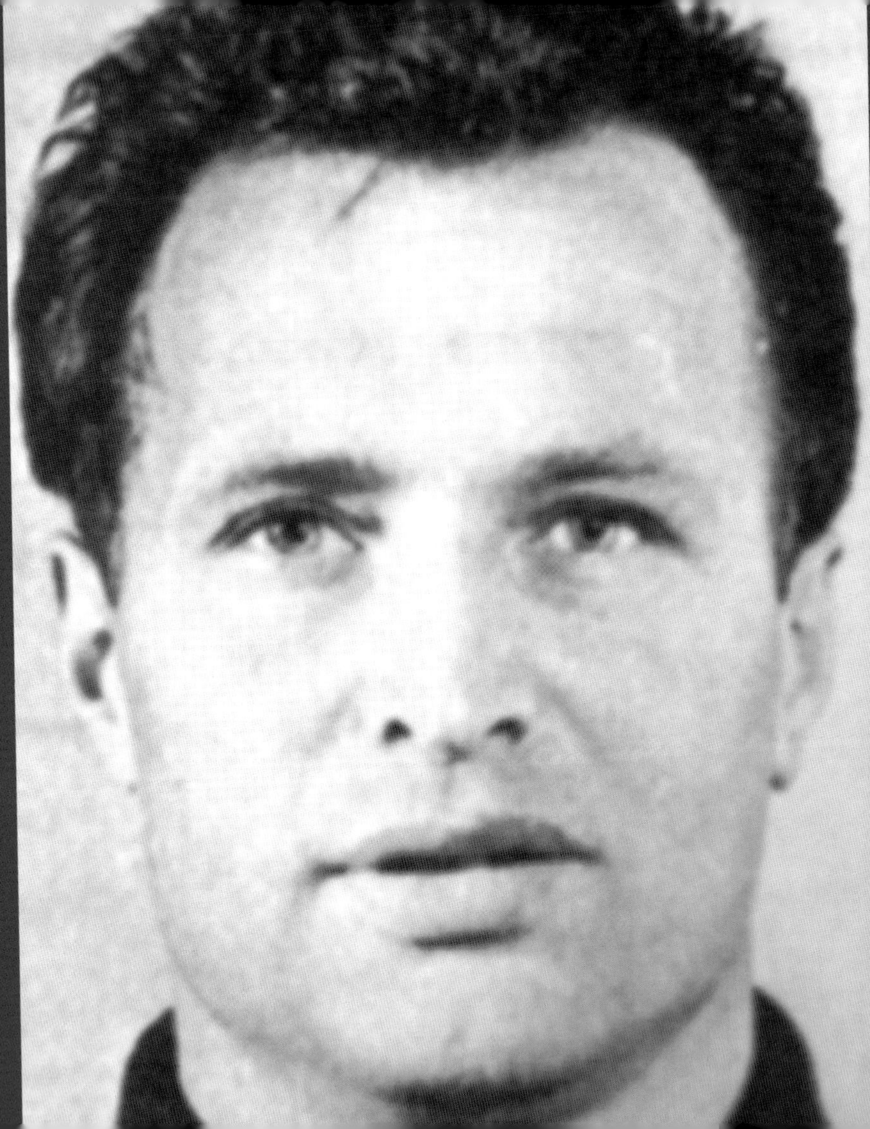

There was never any question of Len White playing out the tail end of his career when he joined County at the age of 34.

White was already a hero in his native North East, following a lengthy career with Newcastle United during which he won an FA Cup winner's medal. He moved to Edgeley Park from Huddersfield Town as a late replacement for Frank Beaumont, who was suspended for County's FA Cup fourth round tie against Bill Shankley's Liverpool.

At Anfield, White scored one of the most famous goals in the club's history, heading County into a shock 1-0 lead. That game would end 1-1 and County would lose the replay, but White had written his name into the County history books. And he didn't stop there, scoring 24 times in 53 League games at the start of the Go Go Go County era.

1960s

Len ALLCHURCH

Welsh wing wizard Len Allchurch was another late arrival at Edgeley Park, making his County debut just six days short of his 32nd birthday. A surprise club record £10,000 move from First Division Sheffield United meant the Welsh international was just in time to take part in the Go Go Go County era of the late 1960s.

In his second season he was a key part of the side that won the Fourth Division championship and would go on to help County perform creditably in their first couple of seasons in Division Three.

His trickery on the wing and his pinpoint crossing perfectly suited strikers Jim Fryatt and Bill Atkins, who were gratefully feeding off his service, scoring 65 League goals between them in two seasons.

1965 - 1969

Johnny PRICE

The diminutive Price dropped three divisions to join County from Burnley in May 1965. Standing only 5ft 3ins tall, the pacy left-winger was the perfect complement to Len Allchurch on the right in County's 1966/67 championship season. The two wingers provided the crosses for strike pair Bill Atkins and Jim Fryatt to convert.

When financial problems led to the break-up of that famous team, Price remained at Edgeley Park until he was sold on to Blackburn Rovers in 1971. He did return for a second stint with County in September 1974 and provided some light in an otherwise dark period for the club.

1965 - 1971, 1974 - 1976

Alan OGLEY

Ogley had a unique relationship with the Edgeley Park crowd in his eight seasons with the club. The popular goalkeeper was frequently serenaded with "Here's to you, Alan Ogley" to the tune of Simon and Garfunkel's *Mrs Robinson*. And he responded, play allowing, by conducting the singing on the Pop Side!

He came to County from Manchester City in an exchange deal that saw young keeper Ken Mulhearn head to Maine Road, after County had won the Fourth Division championship in 1967. It proved a smart move by County, as the instinctive keeper kept guard during some of the club's most troubled seasons.

Ogley's save from Clyde Best in the fourth round League Cup victory over First Division West Ham United in October 1972 was voted Save of the Century at the opening of County's Hall of Fame.

1967 - 1975

Alan Ogley wins the Player of the Year award at
Stockport County.

Ogley at home with his family.

Jim FRYATT and Bill ATKINS

When County launched their Hall of Fame in 2002 they decided to induct strikers Jim Fryatt and Bill Atkins together. It made perfect sense, because Atkins and Fryatt remain forever linked in the minds of supporters as the twin strike force that fed off the service of wingers Johnny Price and Len Allchurch.

Big Bill Atkins played in the final two months of County's 1967 Championship winning side, scoring the header that clinched promotion at Notts County. But the arrival of Jim Fryatt from Torquay United in the October took things to a different plane. Fryatt scored 22 goals in the 32 games he played that season, while Atkins managed 16 goals from 44 games.

Fryatt's departure in a £30,000 move to Blackburn Rovers signalled the start of the break-up of that famous side, with Atkins moving to Portsmouth for £18,000 in March 1969.

 Fryatt: **1967 - 1968**, Atkins: **1967 - 1969**

George BEST

Hatters fans had little to crow about in the Seventies, but at least they got to see one of the greatest footballers of all time pull on a County shirt. George Best played three games for County in November 1975 after being persuaded by manager Roy Chapman to bring some of his footballing genius to Edgeley Park.

Not surprisingly, Best drew the crowds, bringing in 9,240 fans to watch his debut against Swansea City. And he didn't let them down, forcing keeper Steve Potter to direct his inswinging corner into his own net and scoring the third goal of a 3-2 victory himself with a powerful volley.

Playing only in County's home games, Best also scored in his next outing, a 2-2 draw against Watford, but couldn't manage another in his final game – a 1-0 victory over Southport.

Those five points achieved with Best were vital for County, who avoided having to apply for re-election on the final day of the season.

1975

George Best shoots past the Watford
the second of his three appearances fo
on 12 December 1975.

John RUTTER

John Rutter played more than 400 League games for County – all thanks to a letter he wrote at the low-point of his career.

When Exeter City released the full-back following a cartilage operation, Rutter decided to take action and wrote to clubs in his native North West asking for a trial. County were happy to give him his chance, and he never looked back.

Season after season, he was one of the first names on the team sheet of the host of managers he played under at Edgeley Park. He also worked as the club's commercial manager before leaving in 2005 after a 29-year association with the club.

1976 - 1986

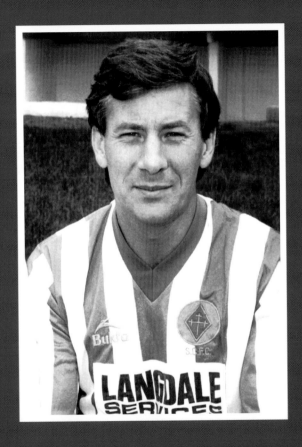

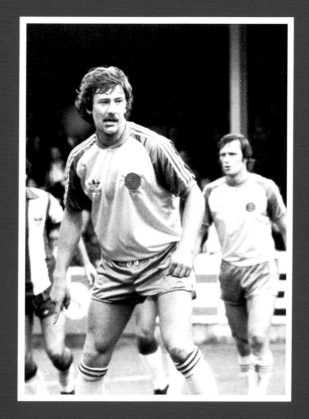

John Rutter in action.

Terry PARK

Many a miserable Friday night at Edgeley Park in the Seventies was brightened by the skill of midfielder Terry Park.

His most memorable moment was a superb solo goal that gave County a 2-1 lead against Manchester United at Old Trafford in the second round League Cup tie on 30 August 1978. Referee Peter Willis ruined County's Cup dream that night with two controversial decisions that allowed United to score twice in the last couple of minutes. But Park had made his name, and in March 1979 he and teammate Ken Fogarty moved to the United States to join Fort Lauderdale Strikers in a £100,000 deal.

Park played another couple of months for County that autumn and returned for good in March 1981. Another 50 games took his total to 181 appearances for the club, scoring 24 goals.

Pictured left: Terry Park jumps for joy after scoring his superb solo goal against Manchester United in the second round of the League Cup at Old Trafford in August 1978.

1976 - 1979, 1981 - 1982

Andy THORPE

In his two spells at the club, the Stockport-born defender amassed 555 appearances – a club record that is unlikely to be broken any time soon.

Thorpe came through the ranks at Edgeley Park and played in every position in defence and midfield when he reached the first team. A shock move to Tranmere Rovers in 1986 was turned around in 1988 when Asa Hartford brought him back to County.

Thorpe was captain when County finally made it out of the Fourth Division in 1991, after a painful 21 years. His final appearance for the Hatters was at Wembley the following year when he came on as sub in the Autoglass Trophy Final against Stoke City.

Thorpe tried his luck in Australia after being released from County, but an Achilles tendon injury curtailed that experiment, and he returned to England for a spell in non-League football and a couple of appearances with Doncaster Rovers. He is currently working as Rochdale's physio.

1978 - 1986, 1988 - 1992

Tommy SWORD

Stepping up from non-League Bishop Auckland in October 1979, Tommy Sword quickly established himself as a cult hero with the County fans. A passionate player, he brought the same enthusiasm for the game whether playing at centre-forward or centre-half.

In his second season with County he suffered a broken leg that kept him out of the game for a year, but returned stronger than ever. Sword became the most successful penalty-taker in the club's history, netting 25 of his 55 goals from the spot in his seven seasons with the club.

A move to Hartlepool in July 1986 was reversed in less than a year for a second short spell with County.

1979 - 1987

Micky QUINN

The burly striker's career really took off at County at a time when he looked set to waste his undoubted talent. Wigan Athletic wanted rid of Quinn so badly in 1982 that they coughed up a special payment to help with his wages at Edgeley Park!

Speedy despite his bulk, Quinn set about proving himself after being dropped by boss Eric Webster early in his County career. He scored 41 goals in 70 games for County, making himself a massive hero at Edgeley Park, before a £52,000 move to Oldham Athletic, and on to further glories with Portsmouth, Newcastle United and Coventry City.

Since retiring from football he has become a professional racehorse trainer with stables at Newmarket, and is a football and racing pundit on Talksport radio.

 1982 - 1984

Bill WILLIAMS

The cultured defender rarely put a foot wrong in his 313 appearances for County – a career which ended at Wembley Stadium in the 1994 Play-off Final against Burnley.

Williams arrived from Rochdale as a converted midfielder and played through both sides of the County story, emerging from the problems under Jimmy Melia to take a full part in the Danny Bergara revival of the Hatters' fortunes.

Manchester City signed Williams in October 1988 for £50,000, but he was back at Edgeley Park just two months later in a £30,000 move. Throughout his time at Edgeley Park he also worked in his father's decorating firm.

1985 - 1994

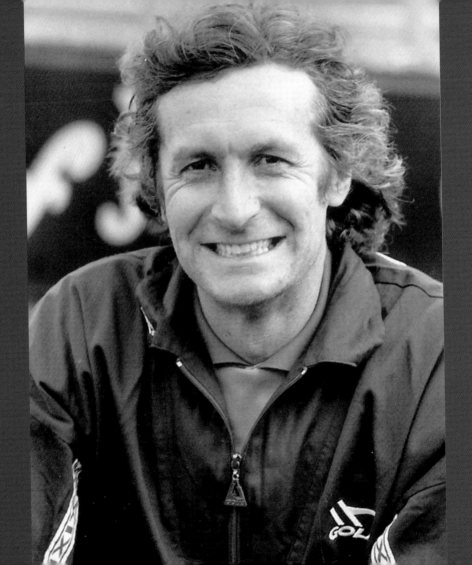

Rodger WYLDE

Rodger Wylde only spent one season on the playing staff at Edgeley Park, scoring 12 goals in his 26 appearances.

But the popular striker stayed on with County after his playing career ended, turning to the physiotherapy he had studied so he could remain in football. He has been club physio for more than 19 years, working under eight different managers. County fans voted him into the club's Hall of Fame in May 2006.

During his playing days he enjoyed successful spells with hometown club Sheffield Wednesday, Oldham Athletic, Sporting Lisbon, Sunderland and Barnsley. He plays guitar alongside former player Tom Bennett in the rock band Fracture.

1988 - 1989

Chris BEAUMONT

Chris Beaumont played in all four of County's Wembley appearances in the 1990s.

The powerful midfielder, who spent a great deal of time out wide, providing service for Kevin Francis and Andy Preece while at County, was a late starter in professional football. He was recommended by Danny Bergara's son Simon, who played alongside him for Denaby United, and the Uruguayan signed him first for Rochdale and then for the Hatters.

The 1993/94 Second Division Play-off Final against Burnley proved the best of times, and the worst of times for Beaumont, who scored an early goal and was then sent off by referee David Elleray in controversial circumstances.

He made more than 300 appearances for County before moving to Chesterfield for £30,000 in 1996 where his versatility and work rate won over the Saltergate fans in the same way they had at Edgeley Park.

 1989 - 1996

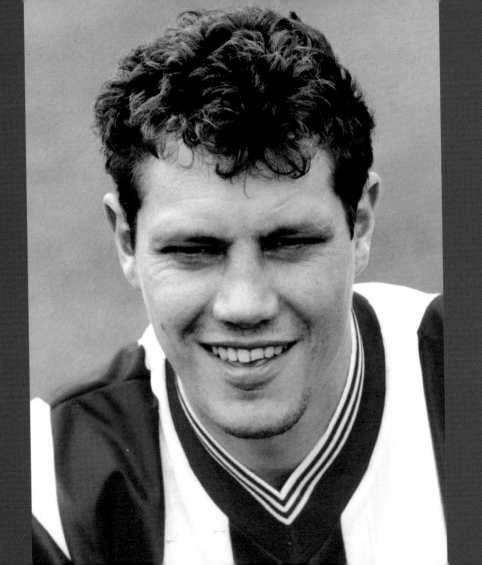

Brett Angell congratulates County's Alun Armstrong on his goal against Gillingham.

Brett Angell was top scorer in each of his four full seasons at Edgeley Park.

The big striker became County's record purchase when Asa Hartford bought him from Derby for £30,000 in 1988. Some fans took some convincing over his awkward style, but under new boss Danny Bergara he managed to finish as the Fourth Division's top scorer as County reached the play-offs in his first season.

A transfer request hardly endeared him to supporters, but after stays at Southend, Everton (a sell-on clause earned County £160,000) and Sunderland, Angell returned to County on loan.

With a permanent £120,000 deal struck, Angell returned to Edgeley Park and his position in County history was secured. In the wonderful 1996/97 season it was Angell who scored the goal at Chesterfield that sent County up into the second tier. He continued to score at the higher level and by the time he left for the second time he had 95 County goals to his name.

1988 - 1990, 1996 - 1999

Grimsby Town's Richard Smith battles with Brett Angell for the ball during the opening
League match of the season against Stockport County at Blundell Park.

Ian Moore congratulates Brett Angell on
his second goal against Crystal Palace.

Angell shoots to score against Huddersfield Town.

Brett Angell gets one of the few chances in County's
match versus Bournemouth that were on target.

Jim GANNON

There's no doubt that Jim Gannon the player is a legend at Edgeley Park. But he strives for legendary status off the field as well.

The big defender's playing career at County lasted 479 appearances, during which time he showed his versatility by switching positions as occasion demanded. He also scored 64 goals, which puts him ninth in the club's scoring records.

All that would have made him one of County's key figures in their 125-year history, but Gannon also happens to be the man who saved County from slipping out of the League. After managing Dundalk in his native Ireland he answered the club's call when Chris Turner resigned following a 6-0 defeat at Macclesfield on Boxing Day 2005.

In his first few months as manager he kept County up when they appeared to be heading for Conference football. At the time of his appointment, County had been five points adrift of safety. In his first full season Gannon put together a side that set a new Football League record of nine consecutive victories without conceding a single goal. Another League record was equalled the next year when County won eight away games on the bounce.

1989 - 2000

Jim Gannon puts pressure on the Wycombe Wanderers'
defence to force an own goal for County's second.

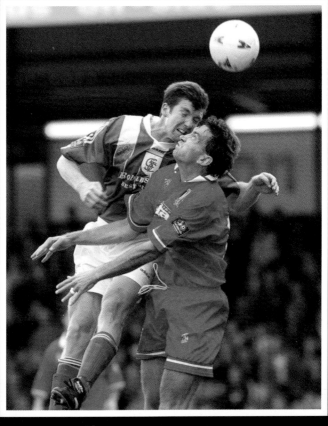

Jim Gannon gets a header past
Gillingham and bound for goal.

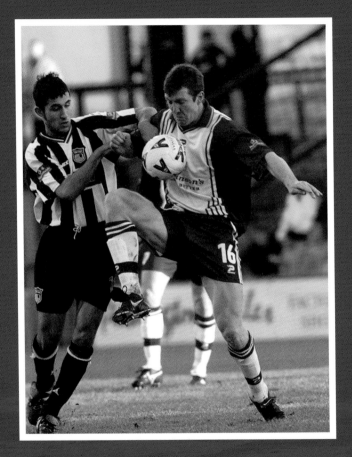

Jim Gannon wins a tackle against Grimsby.

Future County manager Jim Gannon goes for goal in the Autoglass
Final against Stoke City on 16 May 1992 at Wembley.

Lee TODD

Lee Todd was one of the most popular players of the Danny Bergara/Dave Jones era. His determined performances at left-back were always appreciated by the Edgeley Park fans, who voted him into the club's Hall of Fame in 2006.

Todd began his career with hometown club Hartlepool United, before moving to County on a free transfer in 1990. After helping County to promotion from the Second Division in 1997, he followed Dave Jones to Southampton, bringing in a fee of £850,000.

After a year in the Premier League he moved back north for an injury-blighted stay with Bradford City. Spells with Walsall and Rochdale followed, before Todd moved into non-League football with Mossley and Stalybridge Celtic.

A real County man, Todd is a regular visitor to Edgeley Park on match days.

1990 - 1997

1990s

Peter WARD

Ward was a combative midfielder, who brought a real bite to County's midfield in his four seasons at the club in the early 1990s.

Danny Bergara brought Ward, along with a number of other players, from his former club Rochdale after County's promotion from the Fourth Division in 1991. And Ward proved one of his best buys, linking up superbly with David Frain in central midfield as County marched into fifth place in Division Three, losing in the Play-off Final.

He left County for Wrexham in 1995, but returned after his playing career ended to work with County's Centre of Excellence. When Jim Gannon took over as manager in January 2006 he made Ward his assistant manager.

1991 - 1995

1990s

Kevin FRANCIS

The very embodiment of County's rise from Fourth Division mediocrity, Francis provided Danny Bergara's side with their finest target man. At 6ft 7ins tall, Francis was never going to be an ordinary player, but what set "Big Kev" apart was a well-tutored approach to the game that saw him as skillful on the ground as he was troublesome in the air.

After arriving from Derby County for a £45,000 fee, Francis became a focus for opposing fans' jibes, and the occasional TV commentator's mockery, but he appeared to thrive on adversity. In all, he scored 117 goals in 198 appearances, including two of the goals in the 5-0 victory over Scunthorpe that ensured promotion in May 1991, County's first-ever goal at Wembley in the Autoglass Trophy final against Stoke, their second in the Play-off Final against Peterborough a week later, and then a header in the following year's Autoglass Trophy final against Port Vale.

He left for hometown club Birmingham City in January 1995 for a then club record £800,000, but made a brief return under Andy Kilner in 2000 before suffering a serious injury against Manchester City.

At the Gala Dinner to celebrate 100 years of football at Edgeley Park in October 2002, Francis was named 'County Player of the Century'.

1991 - 1995, 2000

Kevin Francis turns away to celebrate after scoring his 100th goal for
County in the 2-1 victory against Port Vale at Edgeley Park in April 1994.

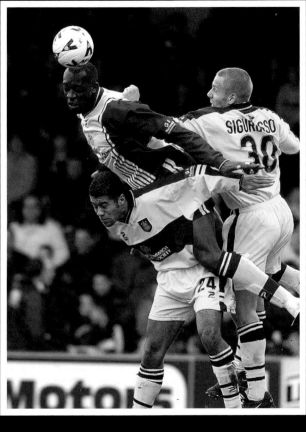

Kevin Francis gets above Blackpool's
Phil Horner to head close.

Blackpool v Stockport: Kevin Francis gets above Phil

The talented right-back, who spent nearly nine years at Edgeley Park, scored one of the most famous goals in the club's history. County were 2-0 down from the first leg of the Coca-Cola Cup semi-final against Middlesbrough in 1997 when Connelly popped up at the Riverside to scare the pants off the Premiership opposition with his first-ever goal for the club.

Connelly had been playing for semi-pro side Hallam FC in Sheffield when Danny Bergara decided to offer him a contract in 1992. From the start, Connelly turned in the sort of steady and assured performances that made him one of the first names on the teamsheet of Bergara and his successors, taking his total of League appearances to more than 300.

With County struggling financially, former boss Dave Jones was allowed to take him to Wolves in 2001. Connelly also played for Tranmere Rovers and Rushden & Diamonds before reuniting with Jones as Cardiff City's physio.

1992 - 2001

Mike FLYNN

"Captain Fantastic" was at the peak of his game when leading County to their highest-ever League finish, ending the 1997/98 season eighth in Division One. The Oldham-born defender's defensive prowess and sheer bravery were an inspiration to all around him.

By the time Flynn had been given the captain's armband for the 1994/95 season, he had already been part of Danny Bergara's team that reached Wembley for the Second Division Play-off Final, which County lost 2-1 to Burnley. He played an incredible 66 games in the dramatic 1996/97 season, leading County to promotion to the First Division and also to the semi-final of the League Cup.

Attention from bigger clubs inevitably arrived – County rejected an £800,000 bid from Birmingham City in 1999, and he later signed a new contract.

When Andy Kilner was sacked as manager, Flynn was one of the favourites to take over, but Carlton Palmer's arrival meant he was sent out on loan to Stoke. Flynn was given a free transfer just ten days before the tenth anniversary of his arival at County. He went on to play for Barnsley, Blackpool and Accrington Stanley.

1993 - 2002

Mike Flynn fights for the ball with Manchester City's Paul Dickov
in the testimonial game for County physio Rodger Wylde.

Stockport County manager David Jones with players Mike Flynn and
Alan Armstrong at a photocall to announce the £1.3 million lottery
handout for a new hat museum in Stockport

Captain Mike Flynn whips off his shirt and
celebrates after the final whistle of the match
against Blackburn Rovers.

Flynn gives Man City's George Weah a taste of things to come.

Alun ARMSTRONG

Alun Armstrong became County's record sale when he moved to Middlesbrough for £1.6 million in February 1998. The fee represented a massive profit for the club, who had bought him for £35,000 from Newcastle United at the start of Danny Bergara's final season.

Armstrong scored on his debut in the 4-1 victory over Cardiff City and never looked back. He was on the scoresheet in the 1996 FA Cup draw at Everton, and again in the replay. The following season saw County promoted from Division Two and reach the semi-final of the Coca-Cola Cup and Armstrong contributed another 13 goals. He had already scored 15 goals the following season when Middlesbrough wrote the massive cheque to take him to the Riverside.

He went on to play for Huddersfield and Ipswich Town and it was while with the Tractor Boys that he scored a header in the 1-0 win over Inter Milan in the home leg of their UEFA Cup before scoring a late penalty in their 4-1 away defeat in the San Siro.

1994 - 1998

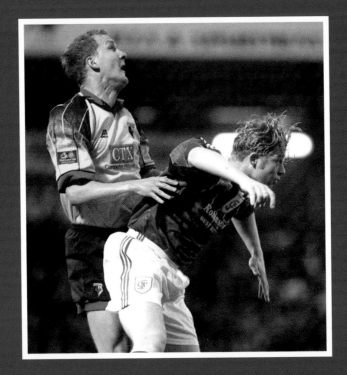

Alun Armstrong in the thick of things against Watford.

Armstrong sets up an attack.

Alun Armstrong is sandwiched between Blackburn Rovers'
Gary Croft and Ian Pearce.

Armstrong goes close with this effort against Brighton.

1990s

Tom BENNETT

Midfielder Tom Bennett quickly became a crowd favourite after joining from Wolves in June 1995. His partnership with Chris Marsden provided County with one of their finest central midfields ever.

Bennett's County career, which included playing all but three games of the historic 1996/97 season, would have surpassed his eventual total of 110 League games but for a horrific injury against Birmingham City.

Bennett broke his leg in five places on a miserable night at St Andrews in January 1998. He was out for more than 12 months, eventually returning in a game at Huddersfield Town in March 1999. He only appeared 15 more times for County before enjoying a successful spell at Walsall before spells with Boston United, Kidderminster Harriers and Hamilton.

Bennett still plays in the band Fracture with County physio Rodger Wylde. The pair set up the group to cheer up Bennett during his lengthy spell out.

Tom Bennett gets in a tackle.

Tom Bennett and Kevin Cooper congratulate Brett
Angell after he scores the winning goal against Bury.

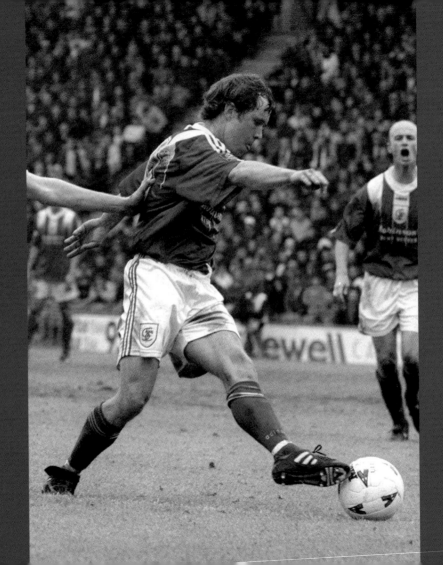

Kevin COOPER

Kevin Cooper was on loan from Derby County when he helped Dave Jones's County gain promotion into the First Division in 1997.

It was no surprise that Jones's successor, Gary Megson, signed Cooper on a permanent deal for £150,000 at the start of the next season, and he was rewarded with some superb performances from the winger. Possibly the best was when he tormented full-back Rufus Brevett in a 2-0 victory over the Premiership-bound Fulham on New Year's Day 2001, when Andy Kilner was in charge.

Cooper could also be relied on to score the odd spectacular goal, which he did during his 173 appearances for the club.

Cooper was sold to Wimbledon for £1 million in March 2001 and then on for the same amount to Wolves the following year where he reunited with Jones.

He followed Jones to Cardiff City and in 2008 joined Chesterfield.

Dave Jones's County squad at the start of the 1996/97 season that would see them win promotion from Division Two and reach the semi-final of the Coca-Cola Cup.
Back row (from left to right) Armstrong, Gannon, Bound, Williams, Paul S. Jones, Edwards, Landon, Dinning, Mike. Middle row: Wylde (physio), Eckhardt, Paul Jones, L. Jones, Searle, Bennett, Jeffers, Connelly, Jakub (youth development manager). Front: Mutch, Durkan, Marsden, D. Jones (manager), Flynn, Ware, Todd.

2000s

Stockport County's 2001/02 Finnish connection. (From left to right) Petri Helin, Jarkko Wiss and Shefki Kuqi.

Jarkko Wiss has won more international caps while playing for County than any other player. When the midfielder picked up his ninth international cap for Finland in 2001, he edged out Martin Nash who played eight times for Canada while at Edgeley Park.

Midfielder Wiss, who had a stop-start County career through injury, was also involved in a moment of history when he and striker Shefki Kuqi came off the bench in Finland's 2001 World Cup qualifier against Greece to join Petri Helin. That game represented the first time County have had three players playing in an international fixture.

All three were brought to County by boss Andy Kilner, who had spent part of his playing career in Scandinavia.

2000s

Luke BECKETT

Luke Beckett won Stockport County fans over from day one with his tireless work for the team, and his ability in front of goal.

He joined from Chesterfield and set about proving himself a lethal finisher in a struggling team. Beckett scored 45 goals in 84 appearances for the Hatters, but it would have been a lot more if he hadn't suffered cruciate ligament damage near the start of the 2003/04 season.

He returned at the end of that campaign, but two months into the next he was sold to Sheffield United for £50,000. Since then he has continued to prove his worth as a goal-scorer in spells with Oldham Athletic and Huddersfield Town.

2001 - 2004

Luke Beckett tries an overhead kick against Notts County.

Beckett celebrates his second goal against
Notts County in January 2003.

Luke Beckett fires in a shot against Cardiff City

Beckett celebrates his goal against Peterborough.

2000s

Ashley WILLIAMS

The central defender became the tenth player to gain international honours while with County. Unfortunately for the Hatters, shortly after winning his first Welsh cap for his appearance against Luxembourg in March 2008, Williams was on his way to Swansea City on loan with a view to a permanent move in the summer.

Departure seemed inevitable after Williams's mature defending had brought in scouts from all over to look at a player who had joined County on a free transfer from Hednesford Town on New Year's Eve 2003.

During his time at Edgeley Park he also won the North West Player of the Year award ahead of Premiership stars. Williams was made County captain at just 23 and rarely put a foot wrong in his five years at the club.

Blackpool's John Murphy tackles
Ashley Williams at Bloomfield Road.

2000s

Liam DICKINSON

By April 2008, Liam Dickinson had achieved the brilliant record of scoring 32 goals in just 57 starts. The big striker was on fire in the second half of the 2007/08 season and his goal tally was well deserved for his work rate and determination.

To arrive in League football must have been especially sweet for Dickinson, who had kicked football into touch for a time after being released by Blackburn Rovers as a 16-year-old trainee. His return to the game meant time in the Manchester League with Irlam MS and Swinton Town before a switch to Trafford and on to Woodley Sports in 2005.

After joining County for £2,000 in December 2005 under Chris Turner, he was given his first-team chance by Turner's successor Jim Gannon. His seven goals that term went a long way to keeping County from slipping into the Conference. After a harder second season, he has come into his own this term following the departure of Anthony Elding.

He also provided one of the biggest laughs at Edgeley Park in recent years, celebrating his winning goal against Darlington in April 2008 by running to the bench and pulling down assistant boss Peter Ward's shorts!

Liam Dickinson celebrates with teammate Michael Raynes after County equalised against Mansfield Town in 2008

Scorer of County's opening goal, Dickinson battles
with Rochdale's Nathan Stanton in March 2008

Liam Dickinson tries a dramatic overhead
kick as Carlisle United look on.

As the Oxford Utd v Orient result comes through, and they realise they will play League football next season, jubilant fans engulf Liam Dickinson in the Cheadle End at Edgeley Park

County's Blue & White Army has long been regarded as the club's 12th man and the fans have now been given that number in the Hatters' squad list. Here the Cheadle End produce a special display before the last game of the 2005/06 season when Jim Gannon's side retained their Football League status with a draw against Carlisle United.

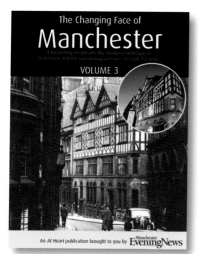

The Changing Face of Manchester Volume 3
£12.99
ISBN 978-1-84547-160-6

The Changing Face of Manchester Volume 3 is a unique collection of nostalgic and evocative images, selected from the archives of the *Manchester Evening News*, illustrating the dramatic changes the city has undergone throughout the decades. Much of the city has changed but many of the beautiful red-brick Victorian facades of city centre buildings remain the same.

Picture of well-known sights through the years show the vivid similarities and differences in familiar places. Whether you have lived in Manchester, or are visiting, this book will present interesting views on the continuing evolution of this vibrant city.

For more information: If you would like any further information on the above title please contact us at the address below.
At Heart Ltd: 32 Stamford Street, Altrincham, Cheshire, WA14 1EY **Tel:** 0161 924 0159 **Fax:** 0161 924 0160

At Heart Ltd Titles

For more information or to buy any of these titles visit **www.atheart.co.uk** or your local bookseller

Lancashire Titles

Pocket Belle Vue	978-1-84547-164-4	£6.99
Manchester At War	978-1-84547-096-8	£14.99
The Changing Face of Manchester Vol. 1 (Revised Edition)	978-1-84547-189-7	£12.99
The Changing Face of Manchester Vol. 2	978-1-84547-104-0	£14.99
The Changing Face of Manchester Vol. 3	978-1-84547-160-6	£12.99
The Changing Face of Manchester in the Seventies	978-1-84547-117-0	£12.99
Around Manchester in the 50s & 60s (Revised Edition)	978-1-84547-192-7	£12.99
Manchester City FC: 125 Years of Football	978-1-84547-185-9	£12.99
Lancashire's Four Seasons	978-1-84547-183-5	£12.99
The Ribble Valley in Pictures	978-1-84547-188-0	£12.99
Blackpool Then and Now	978-1-84547-153-8	£12.99
Legends: The great players of Blackpool FC	978-1-84547-182-8	£12.99
Chorley Past	978-1-84547-136-1	£12.99
Garstang Past	978-1-84547-137-8	£12.99
Wigan Past	978-1-84547-184-2	£12.99

For more information: If you would like any further information on any of the above titles please contact us at the address below.
At Heart Ltd: 32 Stamford Street, Altrincham, Cheshire, WA14 1EY **Tel**: 0161 924 0159 **Fax**: 0161 924 0160